PERGAMON

Vehbi Bayraktar

NET
TURİSTİK YAYINLAR
SANAYİ VE TİCARET A.Ş.

Published and distributed by:

NET TURİSTİK YAYINLAR A.Ş.

Şifa Hamamı Sok., No: 18/2, 34400 Sultanahmet-Istanbul/Turkey
Tel: (90-1) 516 84 67-517 77 34 Fax: (90-1) 516 84 68

236. Sokak No. 96/B Funda Apt., 35360 Hatay-İzmir/Turkey
Tel: (90-51) 28 78 51 Fax: 50 22 73

Kışla Mah., 54. Sok., İlteray Apt. 11/A-B 07040 Antalya/Turkey
Tel: (90-31) 48 93 67-43 14 97 Fax: (90-31) 48 93 68

Eski Kayseri Cad., Dirikoçlar Ap., No: 45, 50200 Nevşehir/Turkey
Tel: (90-485) 130 89-146 20 Fax: (90-485) 140 36

Text: **Vehbi Bayraktar**
Translation: **Nüket Eraslan**
Photographs: **Vehbi Bayraktar, Selim Aydaş** (1,20,22,25,28,71), **Levent Tekeş** (12,75)
Layout: **Not Ajans (Fatih M. Durmuş)**
Typesetting: **Özyalçın Koll. Şti.**
Colour Separation: **Renkler Matbaası A.Ş.**
Printed in Turkey by: **Güzel Sanatlar Matbaası A.Ş.**

ISBN 975-479-014-0

Edition, 1996

Contents

Its Establishment

P ergamon was established on and in the vicinity of the Acropolis hill against which the district of Bergama rests today. The city is bounded by the Cetius river in the east and by the Selinus river in the west. Both rivers join each other to the south of the modern city and drain into the Kaikos (Bakırçay) river. Değirmendere, situated in the Kaikos valley, is the oldest settlement in the region of Pergamon. Excavations at the acropolis itself, revealed prehistoric treasures contemporary with the finds excavated in Değirmendere. Since these were very few in number, many scientists believe that there were no prehistoric settlements on the acropolis.

In Pergamon, nothing belonging either to the period of colonization which had started in the 12th century B.C. and lasted until the 10th century B.C., or to the subsequent period of migrations, was discovered during excavations. Those who came during the period of migrations preferred to settle either on the offshore islands, or on peninsulas that could be defended easily. Since Pergamon was approximately 25 km. inland, it was not a favourable site for settlement. The exact date of its establishment is not knwn. According to mythology, the name Pergamon goes back to the Trojan wars. Following the burning and destruction of Troy, Andromache, the wife of Hector, was enslaved by the Achaeans and married to the son of Achilles, Neptolemus, from whom she had three children. Of these, the one named Pergamos is known as the founder of the city of Pergamon. The name of the city comes from the word "Pergamons". It was modified and changed into Pergamon in the Early Ages and later became today's Bergama. It means a high place, a castle. Perg, berg and amo, are roots that are often encountered in Anatolian languages and they are found in the word Pergamon also.

2- Acropolis, general view.

3- Temenos of Demeter.

Only a few treasures dating back to the archaic period have been discovered in the course of excavations on the acropolis. Since no settlements belonging to the same period have been discovered, the hypothesis that the city was founded in the archaic period has lost its appeal.

According to some scientists, treasures belonging to the archaic period were brought by the Pergamene kings of the Hellenistic era from the coastal cities to decorate their palaces.

We know that by 560 B.C., the whole region came under the rule of Kroisos, the King of Lydia, but a few years later, the Persian king Kyros defeated Kroisos and started to rule Anatolia. Persians divided Anatolia into four main satrapies: Ionia, Hellespont, Cilicia and Lydia. According to the division, Pergamon was included in the province of Mysia in the Lydian satrapy. During the Persian rule, like the other cities, Pergamon enjoyed complete freedom in its internal affairs, but paid heavy taxes and supplied soldiers to the Persian army when requested. Due to the harsh rule of the Persians and the draining of resources because of the wars,cultural and social activities in Pergamon came to a standstill and what was known as the Classical Age came to an end. In the course of excavations, nothing more than a few treasures from the asklepeion, which reflect the beauty and elegance of the period, have been found.

4- Altar of Zeus.

When the famous historian Xenophon (430-352 B.C.),came to Pergamon on his return from East Anatolia (399 B.C.), the widow of Gongylos, Hellas, who was ruling the region, hosted him. Hellas asked Xenophon's help to free the area from the Persian feudal lord Asidates, who owned a farm in the Kaikos region. In return, she promised him the treasures of Asidates. Upon this request, Xenophon sacrificed an animal and had his fortune told. Encouraged by what the fortune-teller had told him, he attacked Asidates' farm with a force of three hundred soldiers, yet had to retreat when the soldiers on the farm signalled for help from the Persian forces in the vicinity by lighting fires. The next day Xenophon pretended to leave Pergamon, but he then made a full-scale attack on the small village where Asidates had taken refuge. He captured the riches of Asidates as well as his wife and children. After his victory, Xenophon returned to Pergamon and sacrificed animals to the gods in gratitude.

In 362 B.C., some of the cities in Anatolia revolted against the Persian king Artaxerxes, and as their leader chose Orontes, the satrap of Mysia who had friendly relations with the King of Athens. Orontes established his headquarters in Pergamon and won many victories over the Persians in the beginning, but later he was defeated.

The Age of Alexander the Great

I n 334 B.C. Alexander the Great, the King of Macedonia, crossed the Dardanelles and came to Anatolia. He fought the Persian king Darius III on the bank of the River Granicus(today's Biga Çayı) and defeated him. Thus, Western Anatolia came under his rule. Alexander chose Barsine, the widow of the Persian commander Memnon (from Rhodes) to administer Pergamon. His decision caused widespread gossip that he was having an affair with Barsine, and that Heracles, who ruled Pergamon in 310 B.C., was born out of wedlock. Upon the death of Alexander the Great in 323 B.C. the empire was divided among his generals, and according to this division, Seleukos received Mesopotamia, Syria and the cities in Eastern Anatolia; Lysimachus received Southern and Western Anatolia; Kassandros received Macedonia and Greece; Ptolemaios received Egypt, Libya and Northern Anatolia.

Lysimachus, realizing the strategic location of Pergamon, turned it into a military base and maintained his superiority. He appointed Philetairos, who was one of the commanders of Antigonos (whose aim it was to capture the whole of Anatolia), the commander of the castle of Pergamon. Philetairos, who had surrendered to Lysimachus, was a diligent and an efficient commander whom Lysimachus favoured so highly that, he entrusted to him the 9,000 talent gold coins which were his share of Alexander the Great's treasury. In order to ensure the expansion of the kingdom, Lysimachus esta-

5- Selinus Stream.

blished diplomatic relations with the other kingdoms in the region and favoured marital ties between the members of the royal families. He married Arsinoe, the daughter of Ptolemaios, and arranged the marriage of his son Agatokles to his sister-in-law.

Arsinoe wanted her own son, not Agatokles to become the king after Lysimachus, so she succeeded in turning Lysimachus against Agatokles and had him murdered. The event caused riots in the army and among the people. Unrest and a feeling of insecurity spread over the land. Agatokles' wife, sister and children sought help from Seleukos, the King of Syria. Also, Philetairos, the commander of the castle of Pergamon, thinking his life was in danger since he was no longer liked by Arsinoe, secretly communicated with Seleukos and told him that if he agreed to attack Lysimachus, he would surrender the treasury to Seleukos. Seleukos accepted the offer and atatcked Lysimachus. He defeated Lysimachus in Koroupedion in 281 B.C.

The Kingdom of Pergamon

T he death of Lysimachus created a throne and a state for Philetairos. Soon after the war, representatives of the Syrian king came
to demand the treasury promised as part of the deal, but Philetairos
refused to part with it. He spent some of the treasury to restore the
city walls of Pergamon and to acquire soldiers. On the new coins he
minted, he had the likeness of Seleukos impressed, thereby show-
ing his allegiance to him. Later, he declared himself "King", and extended the borders of his kingdom as far as the shores of the Sea of
Marmara. The friendly relations he established with the neighbouring kingdoms enabled him to enlarge his territory. Strabon indicates
that Lysimachus' commander Philetairos, who guarded the treasury
of Alexander in the Pergamene acropolis, realized the advantageous
location of the city which could be easily defended, and this intelli-
gent and talented commander opened a new era in the history of
Pergamon.

The Age of Eumenes I (263-241 B.C.)

A s Philetairos did not have a male heir, one of his brothers, either
Eumenes or Attalos, could have ascended the throne. However,
they were quite old, therefore Philetairos preferred to have one of
his nephews inherit the throne. First he adopted his older brother
Attalos' son, but he died before Philetairos. Then he adopted Eumenes, the son of Eumenes and willed him his throne. After his
death, Antiochus, the King of Syria, refused to recognize Eumenes,
and demanded the treasury which had been denied to him during
the reign of Philetairos. Faced with a possible war, Eumenes signed
treaties with every city in Western Anatolia that was against the Syr-
ians. He fought and defeated the Syrian army in the Sardes plain, and
while escaping, Antiochos was killed by a Galatian soldier (261
B.C.). Thus, the Pergamene Kingdom expanded considerably. The
likeness of Philetairos was impressed on the new coins minted. As a result of the newly acquired lands, the Pergamene became neigh-
bours with a warrior tribe, the Galatians, who had settled in the vicinity of the Sangorios (Sakarya) and Halys (Kızılırmak) rivers. In
order to keep the Galatians from attacking them, the Pergamene
paid them tribute.

Eumenes was a just and realistic king. During his time, Pergamon
became a centre of arts and science and competed with the other
cities in Anatolia. He encouraged young Attalos who was a successful athlete, and enabled him to enter the Olympic Games. An inscription discovered in the city states: "Many chariots came from Ar-
gos and Teselia. Attalos' chariot was among these. They lined up behind a stretched rope and when the rope was pulled away, the
horses began to run. The chariot of Attalos, as fast as an arrow, was
leading the others and raising dust. His chariot won the race amid a

shower of applause." Following his victory, a joyous atmosphere prevailed in the city. Archesilas, the poet from Pitane, wrote: "Pergamon, not only for its weapons but for its horses too, deserves praise. If a mortal is allowed to quote the thoughts of Zeus, he may say in the future, Pergamon deserves more fame and honours."

Eumenes I ruled Pergamon successfully for twenty-two years, and he was convinced that Attalos who was going to succeed him would continue in his footsteps.

The Age of Attalos I (241-197 B.C.)

Attalos inherited a large country, a strong and disciplined army and a rich treasury. He considered the tribute paid to the Galatians unfair and ceased to pay. In response, the Galatians gathered in the vicinity of Ankara and attacked the land of the Pergamene to loot and take booty. Seeing the morale of the army decline when none of the principalities offered help, Attalos I secretly wrote in his palm the word Nike (victory) backwards, and made an imprint of it

6- Columns, Temple of Trajan.

on the liver of the animal sacrificed to foretell the outcome of the inevitable war. When he showed the imprint to his soldiers, they believed the trick and with their morale boosted, attacked the Galatians and defeated them. Following the victory over the Galatians, the fame of Attalos I spread everywhere and he acquired the title "King". (Although Philetairos and Eumenes had been declared kings, the title was never firmly established.) The Pergamene referred to Attalos I as "Soter", the saviour. The booty acquired from the Galatians was placed in the courtyard of the Temple of Athena on the acropolis, the goddess Athena was the protectress of Pergamon. A beautiful statue of the goddess was erected next to the booty, and the following inscription is seen on the base of her statue: King Attalos, with the help of Athena, defeated the Tolistoages Galatians near the source of the Kaikos river. The coins (tetradrahmi) minted after the war, bear the head of Philetairos on one face and the head of Athena on the other.

After their defeat in 230 B.C., the Galatians joined the Seleucids and attacked the Kingdom of Pergamon, but they were defeated again and had to retreat to Galatia. Strabon states that following their defeat, the Galatians, who had previously been looting in Anatolia, could not penetrate the borders of the neighbouring states for the next thirty-six years.

During this period, in the Kingdom of Syria, Seleukos II and his brother Antiochos Hierax, were fighting each other for the throne. Taking advantage of the situation, Attalos expanded his borders as far as the Taurus mountains. In retaliation, Antiochos joined the Galatians and started new attacks. In both the wars that took place between the years 229 and 228 B.C., Pergamon was victorious. Following these victories, the construction of the famous Temple of Zeus was begun and the city was embellished with impressive monuments. Also, friendly relations with Rome were established and developed.

7- Aqueducts.

The Age of Eumenes II (197-159 B.C.)

U pon the death of Attalos I, his oldest son Eumenes II ascended the throne. He was well aware of the refined politics his father had pursued, therefore, he followed in his father's footsteps and continued to have friendly relations with Rome. Even in the first few years of his reign he was faced with two dangers. The first was an attack on Pergamon by a large, well organised Galatian army formed by Ortiagon, one of the Galatian princes. He had succeeded in uniting all the Galatians, and he then attacked the Kingdom of Pergamon which he thought was hindering the establishment of a Galatian Kingdom. Eumenes II defeated Ortiagon. The second danger was the ttack by Antiochus III, the King of Seleucids. The cities of Miletus and Erytra sided with Rome and its friendly ally, Pergamon, and resisted Antiochus, whereas the cities of Ephesus, Tralles and Telmassos supported Antiochus. The battle took place on the Manisa plain and the Pergamene army won the war.

The king died in 159 B.C. During his thirty-eight years of rule, he had been very successful both in military and state affairs. His reign was the golden age of Pergamon. Like his father, he demonstrated great efficiency in the affairs of state. He enjoyed discussions with scholars, poets and artists. Pythias, the historian, and Menandros, the philosopher, were some of his chosen friends, and Lechiades, the famous minstrel of the time, never left his side, even in wars. As is evident, Pergamon had become a centre for arts and science. theoretical sciences like philosophy, mathematics, literature and astronomy, and practical sciences like mechanics, ship building, architecture, textile and leather manufacturing, advanced considerably. Strabon states that both the library and the Temple of Zeus were built during this time. The library founded by Attalos I was enlarged and enriched by Eumenes. He also embellished many of the cities under his domain with monuments. The stoa he built in Athens was 127 metres long. The reign of Eumenes was the richest and the most powerful period in the history of Pergamon. The asklepeion was enlarged so that it could serve the patients arriving from every state in the Mediterranean. It became one of the most famous asklepeions of the time. The acropolis rose within the city walls (called Eumenes II city walls) with its eye-catching monuments. Most of the monuments seen today in Pergamon were built during the reign of Eumenes II.

The Age of Attalos II (159-138 B.C.)

A fter the death of Eumenes II, his brother Attalos II became king. Since Attalos II used to take care of state matters when Eumenes was out of Pergamon, he pursued the same type of politics in state affairs. He was known as a strong and able administrator, knowledgeable in military affairs. The Pergamene looked up to him as a superhuman hero. During the reign of Eumenes II, Attalos had become his right-hand man and he was very popular. Even when Eumenes was still alive, Rome had offered him kingship, but Attalos rejected the offer and remained faithful to his brother. This is why his people called him "Attalos Philadelphos" (brother lover).

Rome did not want any of the kingdoms in Anatolia to become strong. She supported Prusias, the King of Bithynia, against Attalos II, thus causing border fights. Attalos II requested Rome to put a stop to these skirmishes. Rome agreed with Attalos and according to the treaty signed, neither side kept more than 1,000 soldiers along its borders. Taking advantage of the treaty, Prusias used a border skirmish as an excuse and attacked Pergamon with all his might. Attalos II took refuge on the acropolis. Prusias looted the lower city, and after a sacrificial ceremony in the asklepeion, he looked at the statue of Asklepios by the sculptor Pyromachus and said, "You belong to my land; you protect it", and had the statue taken to Bithynia.

Later he attacked the coastal city of Elaia in the Kingdom of Pergamon, but he was repelled by Sasandros, the stepbrother of Attalos. While he was retreating to Bithynia, he looted many of the cities along the route. During his retreat, an epidemic killed many of his soldiers, and his fleet in the Mediterranean lost many ships in a storm. After a short while, in revenge, the Pergamene started a strong attack, but Rome intervened and a treaty was signed, forcing Prusias to relinquish the captured lands and withdraw within his pre-war borders.

One of the most important public works projects of Attalos II was the cleaning of Ephesus harbour. The alluvium deposited by the Kaystros river had filled the harbour and rendered it unusable to sea traffic. Attalos had the bottom of the barbour scraped so that big ships could enter. He also built a stoa both in Athens and in Termesos, and founded the city of Attaleia (named after him), today's Antalya.

The Age of Attalos III (138-133 B.C.)

Upon the death of Attalos II, his nephew Attalos III ascended the throne. Except for a brief war with the Bithynians, the reign of Attalos III was uneventful. He did not like to get involved in the affairs of the state and allowed the people he trusted to administer the it. He was interested in biology, zoology, poisons and antidotes, and spent his days doing research and experiments in these fields. In his will, he bequeathed the kingdom to Rome.

His half-brother Aristonikos intervened and started riots. Since he promised freedom to the slaves, he quickly gained supporters, even from the Pergamene army. Some of the cities joined the revolt, but cities like Colophon, Myndos and Samos resisted joining and they were seized by force. While his fleet was in Cyme, it was attacked by the Ephesian fleet and destroyed (Ephesus supported Rome), in spite of the disaster, the revolt spread inland from the coastal cities. In 131 B.C. a Roman army under the command of Consul Licinius Crassus Mucianus came to Anatolia, but was defeated and Mucianus was captured. When Mucianus could not find an opportunity to commit suicide, he stabbed a Thracian soldier in the eye with his cane and the soldier killed him. Therefore, he succeeded in being killed by a soldier. In 130 B.C., another Roman army under the command of Consul Perperna came to Anatolia and defeated Aristonikos. He was taken to Rome where be was murdered.

The Roman Era

According to the will of Attalos III, Pergamon and the other cities were going to remain independent but render their source of income to Rome. The first clause of the will stated that the private property of the kingdom, its crown, its treasury and its lands would be given to the people of Rome. According to the Romans, this meant that the whole country was the emperor's property and they claimed Pergamon along with the rest of the land. In 129 B.C., Consul M. Aquilla came to Pergamon with ten senators to organise af-

8- Gymnasium-general view.

fairs, and started working form a new type of administration and establish its extent. The will was interpreted wrongly and the state's treasury was sent to Rome. On the land of the ex-kingdom of Pergamon, the first Roman state (Provincia Asia) was established. Riots continued until the reign of Emperor Augustus, when finally peace and tranquility were achieved. Augustus visited Pergamon in the years of 31 and 20 B.C. Encouraged by the warm feelings the emperor had towards them, the Pergamene asked him for permission to build one temple for the emperor and another one for Rome. The exact locations of the Temple of Augustus and the Temple of Dea Roma are not known. Pergamon thus received the great honour of being a Neokoros (having the right to build an imperial temple). In the inscriptions written after Emperor Augustus gave his permission, the word Neokoros precedes the word Pergamon. In 14 A.D. upon the death of Emperor Augustus, Tiberius became emperor. Pergamon, along with many of the other cities in Western Anatolia, was destroyed during the earthquakes in 17 A.D. Tiberius helped these cities and relieved them of the burden of paying taxes.

Emperor Trajan also gave Pergamon permission to build an imperial temple in his honour, and the Pergamene built the Temple of Trajan on the most prominent section of the acropolis; the temple is being restored. In the years of Emperor Hadrian (117-138), the city was reconstructed and it regained its old vitality. The temple built for the Egyptian gods (known as the Red Courtyard) was constructed in this period. The Asklepeion was modernized and it became the most famous hospital in the world.

The plague swept through Pergamon in 166 A.D. An inscription discovered near the Temple of Zeus states: "Oh, great Zeus, chase away the epidemic that is destroying our city of Asklepios". During his return from the Thrace campaign, Emperor Caracalla had a serious accident in Gallipolu and came to Pergamon to be treated in the Asklepeion. Following his recovery, in gratitude, he supported the temples in the city. He had the Temple of Dionysus, located on the terrace of the theatre, plated with marble. After that, the Pergamene referred to him as the "New Dionysus". During this period, the city expanded rapidly on the plain at the foot of the acropolis and trade and industry progressed. Also, the population of the city increased to 150.000.

The Byzantine Era

After the crucifixion, St. John came to Ephesus with the Virgin Mary, and in spite of his old age, he tried to spread the new religion in Ephesus and the other cities in Anatolia. He found followers in Pergamon and in Smyrna (İzmir) during this time when there was

9- Main street.

extreme opposition to the new religion. Later he was taken to Rome where he was tortured. From Rome he was exiled to the island of Patmos, where he wrote the Apocalypse. As stated in the Apocalypse, an Asian church was established in each of the following cities: Ephesus, Smyrna, Pergamon, Sardes, Philadelphia, Tytria and Denizli. St. Paul wrote about these seven churches he had established in Anatolia and about the Christian population of Pergamon. Since Pergamon was a polytheist city before Christianity, and since Christians had been tortured here, St. John called Pergamon "the devil's throne".

In the third century when the gladiators and wild animal fights were quite popular, Emperor Decius had three Christians thrown to the wild animals in the amphitheatre. There was strong reaction to the incident. During the reign of Emperor Diocletianus, Pergamon was just a small Christian city in the Asian province, but in the reign of Theodosius (379-395) however, it became one of the four metrapoli (Ephesus, Smyrna, Tralles, Pergamon) in the province. In the Byzantine era, Pergamon lost its old fame and superiority, and it was united with the Ephesian patriarchate.

In the 7th and 8th centuries, Pergamon, like the other Byzantine cities in Anatolia, was attacked both from land and sea, and therefore decreased in size. Most of the city walls we see today were constructed then. The city weakened under the Arab attacks from the sea. In the 12th century, the settlements on the acropolis and in the Cetius valley were very small compared to their sizes in the Hellenistic and the Roman eras. When the Turks came to the area in the 14th century, they found a small Christian community here. Since the city was located on a road stretching into Central Anatolia, it soon regained its vitality. During the period of peace between the Seljuks and the Ottomans, trade improved and the city became steadily wealthier. Both the Seljuk and the Ottoman religious and public buildings are preserved as monuments in the modern city of Bergame today.

The Excavations

The day Carl Humann, who was in charge of the construction of the Istanbul - İzmir railway, saw a fragment of a frieze brought to him by one of his workers, marks the beginning of the period of excavations in Pergamon. Humann took the fragment to Berlin and showed it to the curator of the museum, Alexander Conze, who immediately recognized the importance of the fragment. A year after, permission to excavate was obtained from the Ottoman administration, and in 1877 they started to excavate where the fragment had been discovered, at the altar of Zeus. In the following years, the Temenos of Athena, the Theatre, the Upper Agora, the Temple of Dionysus and the Royal Palaces were excavated. Many statues and small finds unearthed were taken to Berlin.

In 1900, Wilhelm Dörpfel took charge of the excavations. Until 1913 he excavated the Gymnasium, the Temenos of Hera, the Lower Agora, the House of Attalos and the Temenos of Demeter. He also examined a few of the tumuli to the south of Pergamon.

Between 1927-1938 excavations were carried out under the supervision of Theodor Wiegad. He excavated the Arsenals at the northern end of the acropolis as well as the imperial cult Heroon and its vicinity, and the Temenos of Demeter. Upon the orders of Atatürk and as a result of the relentless efforts of Osman Bayatlı, the treasures unearthed were collected at Bergame and a museum was founded to display the treasures.

In 1957, Erich Boehringer took charge of the excavations, and unearthed the Temple of Asklepios and its vicinity, a section of the Lower Agora and the house nearby. Since 1972, Dr. Wolfgang Radt has been in charge of the excavations and he has excavated the sacred Kapı Kaya (Rock Gate) to the north of Pergamon, as well as the houses and the public buildings located on both sides of the street leading from the acropolis to the city on the plain. He has also started the restoration of the Temple of Trajan.

Since 1977, the pottery-makers' district and the potteries located on the banks of the Cetius river that runs to the east of the Pergamene acropolis, have been excavated under the supervision of Selahattin Erdemgil for the Ministry of Culture and Tourism.

The city of Pergamon spreads over an area of 6 sq.km. and the excavations carried out during the last one hundred years have unearthed only 2-3% of the city. Excavations of the New Theatre, the Amphitheatre and the Stadium, which are but a few of the most important onuments of the Roman era, have not started yet.

10- Theatre terrace.

The City Walls and the Settlement

T he oldest city walls in Pergamon date back to the 4th and 5th centuries B.C. A small section of the city walls can be seen on the highest point of the acropolis. The Arsenals, located at the far nothern end, the Royal Palaces and the Temenos of Athena, were surrounded by these walls constructed of polygonal stones. The main gate of this area resembling a small fortress, was located to the south of the Temenos of Athena, at the site of the gate to the area called the "Inner Fortress" today. A square tower on its eastern side used o protect it.

These walls were rebuilt and extended southward during the reign of Philetairos (281-263 B.C.), when the Pergamene declared their independence, to defend themselves against any attacks, especially those from the Seleucids. The walls located to the north of the Temenos of Demeter and the Gymnasium belong to this period. According to Strabon, the city walls were changed and rebuilt many times, and the final restoration took place during the reign of Eumenes II, when they were extended in the south down to the foot of the hill. The area of settlement surrounded by these walls was 222 hectares. The walls were reinforced by towers erected close to each other. However, towers were not built in the north and in the east where the land sloped steeply. There are no traces of city walls in the south-west and west. During the Roman era, while the city was ex-

11- City walls.

12- Column Capitals, Temple of Trajan.

13- City walls.

panding south-west towards the foot of the acropolis, the city walls were torn down and the stones were used in the construction of new buildings. The bridge (only the remains can be seen today) on the Selinus river, used to connect to the gate on this side of the city. The walls built during the reign of Eumenes had gates in the east, north and south. The one in the south was considered the main gate, and it was a beautiful example of the gates with courtyards of the Hellenistic era. Its foundation is seen near the German house situated at the beginning of the asphalt road ascending to the acropolis and its rectangular courtyard in the centre is surrounded by high walls and three towers. The road reaching the city passes through this gate and extends to the acropolis, making a wide "S". The courtyard has two gates one of which is for pedestrians. In the Hellenistic era, gates with courtyards were used in just about every city as the main defence element. Since gates were the weakest points in the walls, courtyards with towers were built. If the enemy succeeded in penetrating through the gates, it was annihilated by a counter-attack from the high walls and the towers.

During the time of the Pergamene Kingdom, the city grew steadily. Every king and queen built new buildings. By the second century B.C. the city consisted of two sections: at the peak was the Upper City, and half-way down the slope and at the foot, was the Lower City. The city was administered and defended from the Upper City. The garrison and the arsenals were at the northernmost point, the palace which was the administrative centre was located in the east, and the religious buildings and the theatre were located in the west. The main street which ran through the centre of the city, separated the religious buildings from the administrative and military buildings. The Upper City was built on sets and spread out like a fan around the theatre. The people lived in the Lower City, where the agora, the gymnasium and the temenos of Demeter formed a complex. The arsenals and the garrison located at the peak were surrounded by a separate fortress.

14- Tower, late period.

15- City walls.

The city was built on levelled natural terraces and the land was never altered in any way. The main street started at the Eumenes II Gate in the south and wound up to the peak. It followed the lie of the terraces and passed either by or near the larger buildings. Narrow side streets or roads with steps connected the other buildings to the main street.

One or two-storeyed stoas and galleries were constructed on the terrace walls which were built to gain more usable land. These stoas and galleries constituted the main architectural feature of the city.

The Heroon (Imperial Cult Building)

The remains seen on the left of the concrete road that stretches from the parking lot on the Acropolis towards the upper fortress, belong to the Heroon (a mausoleum for heroes), built to honour Attalos I (241-197 B.C.) and Eumenes II (197-159 B.C.). In the Hellenistic era, heroes were revered even after they died. In time, they were cleansed of their mortal sins, were attributed god-like and supernatural qualities, and were worshipped by the building of Heroons for them.

The Heroon is a complex that consists of a peristyle (courtyard) surrounded by cult rooms and rooms used for other purposes. Marble columns with Doric capitals surround the peristyle. On the eastern side, there are thick pillars instead of columns. Behind these, there was a large hall where everybody dined together during the cult ceremonies. The cult room located to the east of this hall measures 6 by 2 metres, and its eastern wall has a niche for the cult sta-

16- Heroon.

17- Heroon, general view.

tue. In the Roman era, the structure, especially the cult room, was altered. The room was enlarged to 12 by 13 metres, a narrow podium was added on to the wall with the niche and the walls were covered with marble. The height of the walls was increased in proportion to the width of the room, and columns with Corinthian capitals were erected on top of the walls to make the room appear two-storeyed. Thus, the cult room resembled a tower with columns.

In the course of excavations, it was discovered that there had been another Heroon and houses at the same site. An inscription unearthed, states that one of these houses belonged to the civil servant in charge of the waterworks in the city. Water pipes and cisterns were also discovered near the house.

Reconstruction of the Heroon.

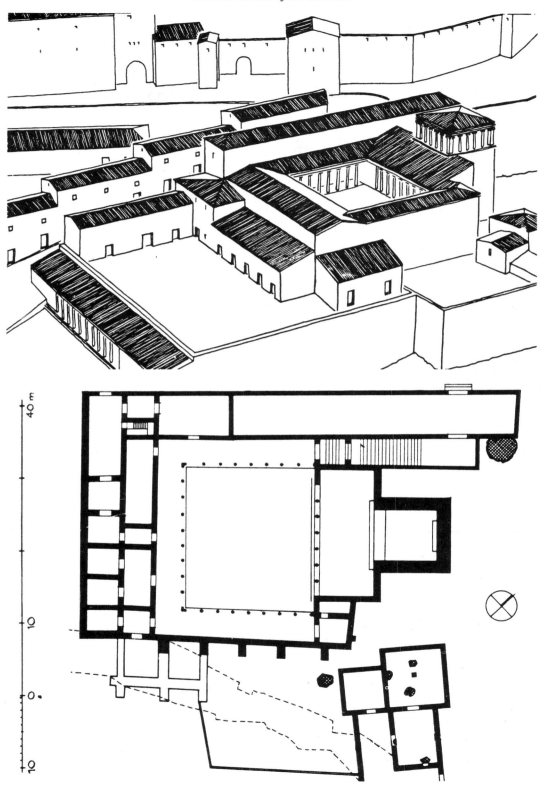

Plan of the Heroon
29

The Royal Palaces

T he concrete road that climbs from the parking lot on the acropolis, runs as far as the gate of the Upper Fortress. The gate has
collapsed and only its eastern tower is standing. The tower was built
of local andesite,and exhibits high quality workmanship. Until the
late Byzantine period, the walls which extended from the tower had
been repaired carelessly many times, using different techniques and
materials. Upon entrance through the gate, on the left are the Temenos of Athena and the Temple of Trajan, and on the right, all along
the city walls, are the Royal Palaces, the foundations of which can be
seen today. These palaces were destroyed in Roman times when a
section of the settlement acquired a religious character. Particularly
during the construction of the Temple of Trajan, the palaces were
torn down and a section of the side rooms was left under the temple. Peristyle houses were very popular in the Hellenistic era and al-
most every house in Pergamon had a peristyle. Although the palaces
were damaged more than the other houses on the acropolis, their
floor plans could be distinguished. The palaces consisted of a small
peristyle measuring approximately 40 by 50 metres or less, surrounded by living rooms, dining-rooms, bedrooms and side rooms
for the servants. As can be detected from the remains, the interior
walls of the palaces were covered with frescoes and mosaics, but the
exterior walls were plain. There were no windows, and sunlight entered through the open peristyle. Since this was not adequate, some

18- Cistern.

of the rooms were quite dark. These palaces were dated according to the finds unearthed. It has been discovered that, at the top of the hill was the palace of Philetairos, the founder of the Kingdom of Pergamon. In the years following his reign, this section of the acropolis was turned into a garrison and the palace of Philetairos was used as a barracks. A row of rooms was built between the palace and the eastern city walls when the palace was turned into a barracks. Only the foundation of these rooms are extant today. In the course of excavations, remains of weapons were discovered in this row of rooms.

The palaces of Attalos I, Eumenes II and Attalos II, are seen in a row along the road with steps,in front of the palace of Philetairos. The palace located at the southern end is the most attractive. A fragment of a cachet which had been made for the altar of Zeus in Pergamon was discovered during excavations at the palace. According to this fragment the palace was dated to 160 B.C. An altar in the north-eastern corner, and a mosaic signed by Hephaistos in the room in the north-eastern corner,were unearthed in the palace.

The tower of the city walls which extended eastward from the palaces is located here. It is still not known for what purpose the open land next to the tower was used. Today, there is a contemporary building here. Since this is the point where the aqueducts from the north reached the fortress, it is possible that the buildings used for the distribution of water in the city were located here. As a matter of fact, a well-preserved round water tank was discovered on the site.

The Arsenals (Military Installations)

From the royal palaces,a narrow lane leads to a complex of five buildings constructed parallel to each other at the northern end of the fortress. These are the arsenals. Their upper storeys have collapsed; only their substructures are extant. The substructures were reinforced with closely built walls parallel to each other, thus creating a grated appearance. Therefore, the substructures were well ventilated and provisions could be preserved for a long time. Food, as well as weapons and ammunition,were stored in these buildings. The thirteen different sized stone shots exhibited in the Lower Agora today were discovered in the course of excavations at the arsenals. These shots, hurled by the catapults placed on top of the city walls, were used in wars to repel the enemy. The arsenals built in the second and the third centuries B.C., were the oldest ammunition and provisions depots of ancient times. This type of depot was found in the headquarters of the legions during the Roman Empire.

19- Temple of Trajan, general view.

The Aqueducts

Supplying water to the city of Pergamon, which was perched on a hill 300 metres high, had been a problem for many centuries. The cisterns dating to pre-Hellenistic times satisfied the demand for some time, but after the expansion of the city during the Hellenistic era, they were no longer adequate. In the second century B.C., water was brought to the city from the springs found at an altitude of 150 metres on the Madra mountain 44 km. to the north. Three different aqueducts brought water from the springs, to the storage room on a 376 metre high hill located to the north of the acropolis. From here, the water was distributed to the acropolis via lead pipes. More than 200,000 baked clay pipes, each measuring 50 to 75 cm. in length and 16 to 19 cm. in diameter, brought water from the springs to the storage room. The three ducts drained water at a rate of 45 litres per second. The aqueducts seen at the northern end of the arsenals were constructed in the second century A.D.. During the Roman

Empire, the city expanded more and spread down toward the plain. In order to satisfy the increased demand for water, another aqueduct was built all the way to the Soma district. Water from the Kaikos (Bakırçay) spring in Soma, was brought to the city by a 53 km. long canal through aqueducts and tunnels. The average diameter of the canals was 90 cm. According to the observations made on the topography of the land, the aqueducts constructed on the Ilyas stream must have been 550 km. long and 40 metres high, making them amongst the most impressive aqueducts in the world. Today, only a small section of these aqueducts is standing.

The devastating earthquake in 178 A.D. damaged the aqueducts of Pergamon. Following the earthquake, a reversed-siphon tower was constructed on the remaining lower storey of the aqueduct that came from the Madra mountain. The route of the canals coming from Soma was changed, and in many places along the route, aqueducts were removed and tunnels were opened. A few of these tunnels ran along the western foot of the acropolis and reached the Lower City. It is assumed that the water coming from Soma entered the town at the northern end of the palaces. Water used to be collected in a depot here and then distributed to the different sections of the city through smaller sized baked clay pipes.

20- Temple of Trajan, general view.

The Temple of Trajan and the Imperial Cult

The marble edifice located to the west of the royal palaces is the Temple of Trajan. During the Roman Empire it was a great honour for a city to possess an imperial temple. Since it was difficult to obtain the emperor's permission to build a temple, the main cities in the empire always tried hard to get that permission and therefore become a neokoros. Pergamon competed with Ephesus and Smyrna (İzmir) and never spared any expense or effort to attain the honour. Emperor Augustus gave his permission to build an Augustus cult centre in Nicomedia in the Bithynian Province and in Pergamon in the Asian Province, on the condition that the centres would be built along with a temple for Dea Roma (the Roman goddess) who already had a temple in Pergamon. The temples were built for the non-Roman citizens of the provinces. After the death of Emperor Augustus, the Pergamene were faced with the danger of losing the neokoroship and therefore their prestige among the Ephesians and the Smyrnians. The Pergamene tried hard for a long time to obtain the permission of the new emperor and finally got it from Emperor

21- Temple of Trajan, foundation.

22- Columns, Temple of Trajan.

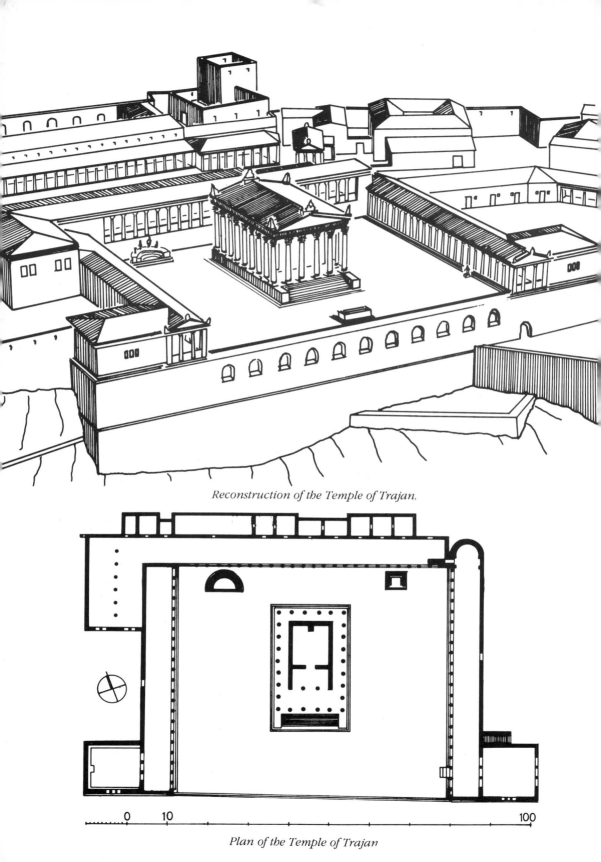

Reconstruction of the Temple of Trajan.

0   10   100

Plan of the Temple of Trajan

23- Columns, Temple of Trajan.

Trajan. Unfortunately, when Emperor Trajan died in 177 A.D. before the completion of the temple being built in his honour, the Pergamene were faced with the same problem. Emperor Hadrian who ascended the throne was quite understanding and declared the permission still valid. Upon the completion of the temple, the Pergamene erected a statue of Emperor Hadrian along with that of Emperor Trajan. Certain fragments assumed to be parts of these statues have been unearthed during excavations. Having an imperial temple in Pergamon was more of a matter of prestige than a matter of religion. Imperial cults never developed into religions.

The Temple of Trajan is situated on the most attractive site on the acropolis, and could be seen from everywhere in the city which spread on the plain during the Roman times. The site of the temple is a "V"-shaped, steep cleft. In order to level the ground where the temple and its temenos were situated, the land was raised by arched and vaulted substructures. The excavation of the foundation revealed that there had been houses at this site before the temple was built. The side rooms of the royal palaces used to be located on the east side of the site. The temple, standing on a high podium, is directed towards the city in the plain. Since most of the edifices on the acropolis were built of either grey or pale pink andesite, the Temple of Trajan which was built of white marble could be seen easily from a distance.

The temple is a peripteros and has 6 by 10 columns with Corinthian capitals. Its three sides are flanked by stoas. In the north, the bases of the columns were raised five metres to create a more monumental appearance when viewed from below the hill. At the western end of its northern portico there was an apsidal niche and a statue base, and at the eastern end there was a statue base, but today only the foundations of these are visible. The temple is being restored according to its original plan.

The Temple of Athena

The Temple of Athena is situated on the wide terrace above the theatre. It is the oldest known temple in Pergamon and was built in the 4th century B.C. It has 16 Doric columns; 6 on the short side and 10 on the long side. Today, only the foundation of the temple is extant. It was a peripteros and its cella consisted of two sections. The two-stepped crepidoma measured 12.72 by 21.77 metres and surrounded the temple made of andesite. Its columns were slender and tall and there were three metopes for every two columns. The fragments of the columns and the architraves have been taken to Berlin.

Following his victory over the Galatians, Seleucids and Macedonians, Eumenes II built the two-storeyed columned galleries at the northern and the eastern sides of the temple. The entrance is on the east side through the two-storeyed columned propylon located by the street. In Berlin the gate was reconstructed using the fragments unearthed during the excavations. According to this, just like the galleries on the sides, the lower columns of the propylon were of the Doric order and the upper ones were of the Ionic order. The space between the two columns in the middle was wider than the others. The inscription on the architrave between the two storeys states "From King Eumenes to Athena who bestowed on him the victory".

24- Temenos of Athena.

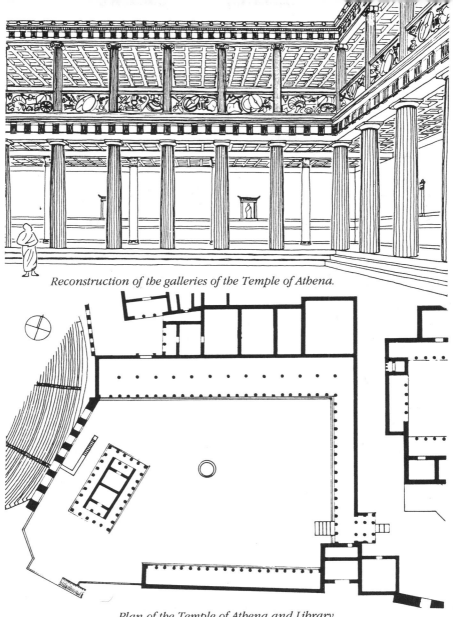

Reconstruction of the galleries of the Temple of Athena.

Plan of the Temple of Athena and Library.

The first floor of the northern gallery is divided into two by a row of columns in the middle. There are niches in the rear wall of this gallery. According to Plinius, statues and reliefs created in Epigonos, Phyromachios Stratonikos and Antigonos, used to stand in these niches. Reliefs depicting the weapons of the Galatians were placed between the columns in the second storey, and these too had been created by the same artists. It is said that later, the bronze statue of Emperor Augustus was erected on the round marble base situated in the middle of the temple. The weapons and the ammunition taken as booty from the Galatians used to be diplayed on the other base next to it.

25- Theatre, Pergamon.

The Pergamon Library

According to Strabon, the library used to be located next to the northern gallery of the temenos of Athena. It must have opened directly onto the second storey of the gallery because there was neither a street nor a square in the vicinity. Its windows and door faced the gallery, and illumination was achieved through there. The library was built by Eumenes II and it consisted of four consecutive rooms. The room at the eastern end is the largest one and measures 13 by 16 metres. It was used as a reading-room. The holes where the wooden bookshelves were mounted can still be seen today. As in most of the other libraries built in ancient times the side walls were double-layered. The space between the layers protected the books from humidity.

The statue of Athena which today is displayed in the Berlin Museum, used to stand on the pedestal seen by the northern wall of the reading room. Including the pedestal, the statue measures 4.5 metres in height and is similar to the Athena Patenos statue in Athens. The height of the statue indicates that the room was 6 metres high. In the other rooms there is no indication of the presence of bookshelves. Ancient sources state that there were 200,000 books in the Library of Pergamon. Since it seems impossible to store that many books in this building it is assumed that there were additional buildings in the vicinity. When relations between Pergamon and Alexandria in Egypt deteriorated, papyrus became scarce in Pergamon and the Pergamene invented parchment paper. The word "parchment" evolved from the word Pergamon.

The Theatre and the Temple of Dionysus

Three monumental theatres were built in Pergamon at different times. The most important theatre is the one which was built on the acropolis in the Hellenistic era. The theatre, situated between the temenos of Athena and the terrace to the west of it, was altered during the Roman Empire. It extends upward like a fan. The cavea where the audience sat is divided into three by two landings (diazoma). The theatre could accommodate 10,000 spectators. The imperial box made of marble is located in the lower section. The other seats are made of trachyte and andesite. A wall with arches and niches was built after the highest row of seats where the theatre borders the temenos of Athena, to improve the accoustics and to achieve a monumental appearance; the southern section of the wall is still standing today. This wall, the imperial box and the stone podium of the stage building, were built during alterations in the Roman period. The orchestra where the chorus stood and the stage building, were situated in the flat area called the "theatre terrace" in front of the theatre.

As in most of the Hellenistic theatres, the stage-building and its podium in the front were made of wood. The grooves seen in situ were where the thick wooden supports holding up the stage building used to be fitted. Since the stage building obstructed the view of the facade of the Temple of Dionysus located at the northern end of the terrace, at the end of each play the building used to be dismantled.

The theatre terrace resembles a narrow hallway 250 metres long. Colonnades and shops used to occupy both sides of it. The gallery in the west used to have a basement on the side facing outward. It is assumed that the wooden parts of the stage-building were stored in a section of this basement. The entrance to the theatre was located at the southern end. It was a monumental gate with three passageways. Nothing is left of the gate.

The Temple of Dionysus was built in the small area at the northern end of the terrace. Since the plays originated from the ceremonies and celebrations held for Dionysus, naturally the temple was built very close to the theatre. Similar examples were discovered in many of the cities of the Early Ages. It may be assumed that traditional sacrificial ceremonies took place before the plays were performed in the temple. The temple which was built in the second century B.C. is a prostylos in the Ionic order. Local andesite was used in the original construction. On his way to Pergamon from Thrace, Emperor Caracalla was in a serious ship accident in Gallipoli and came to the asklepeion in Pergamon for treatment and regained his health. In gratitude, he helped the asklepeion and had his statue erected. He also had the temple plated with marble. After this he was referred to as the "New Dionysus" in Pergamon. The head of the statue in the asklepeion has been discovered and it is on display in the Bergama Museum.

Reconstruction of the Theatre and the Temple of Dionysus.

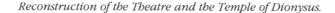

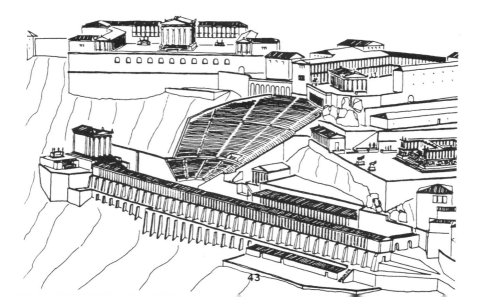

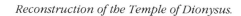

Reconstruction of the Temple of Dionysus.

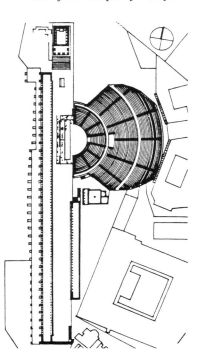

26- Temple of Dionysus.

The Altar of Zeus (the Great Altar)

The Altar is situated to the south of the temenos of Athena on a terrace lower than that of the temenos. Its propylon is to the east of the 70 by 77 metre platform on which it stands. The structure could be viewed in all its magnificence from the Selinus valley in the west, the Cetius Valley in the east and from the Lower City. It is the most important monument on the acropolis dating from the Hellenistic era. It was constructed in the golden age of the Pergamene Kingdom during the reign of Eumenes II. In 190 B.C., following their victory over the Galatians, it was built in gratitude to Zeus and Athena. In 1871, the German engineer Carl Humann, quite by accident, discovered some of its architectural elements and parts of its high reliefs in the Heroon, Upper Agora and along the Byzantine city walls. In the following years, many other fragments were discovered and taken to Berlin where the altar was reconstructed. Today, only the foundation of the altar is seen on the acropolis.

27- Altar of Zeus.

Reconstruction of the Altar of Zeus.

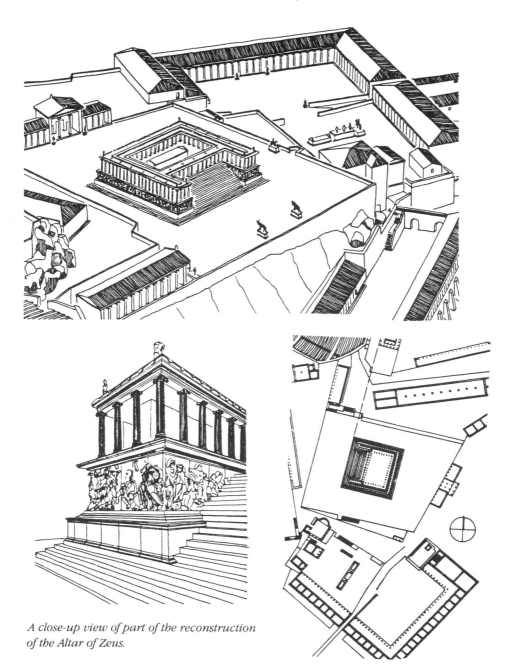

*A close-up view of part of the reconstruction
of the Altar of Zeus.*

Plan of the Altar of Zeus.

28- Altar of Zeus.

The altar had three parts: a five-stepped crepidoma, a base with a frieze and a columned gallery. The horseshoe-shaped altar faced west where twenty steps led up to the main altar in the main area surrounded by colonnades. The white marble altar measured 36.44 by 34.21 metres. When viewed from the side, the five-stepped crepidoma, the base of the frieze, the high relief frieze at a height of 2.3 metres, and the colonnade in the Doric order could be seen. The floor of the colonnade extended out. The most interesting feature of the structure was the 120 metre-long frieze on the exterior. It is the most beautiful example of sculpture in the Hellenistic period. The main theme depicted on the frieze is the victory of the Olympic gods over the Giants and the underworld forces. In the east, associated with sunrise, Apollon, Artemis and their mother Leto, along with the reliefs of Athena and Zeus are depicted. In the north, the goddess of the stars, Orion, the goddesses of destiny, the Moiras, and the goddess of the night are depicted. The gods Oceanos, Amphitrite, Nereus and Triton, all associated with the sea, are depicted in the west. Dawn, Helios the sun god, and other semi-gods are depicted on the south side. Therefore, the reliefs of gods and semi-gods associated with different directions encircled the altar. These were some of the best artistic creations of Hellenistic sculpture. Different periods in the life of Telephos, the son of Heracles, up to the time of his foundation of Pergamon, are depicted on the main altar inside.

It is quite interesting to have all the gods and goddesses of the Early Ages depicted in the same frieze. In this respect, it resembles the Hittite rock-relief in Hattusas where all the Hittite gods were depicted in the same frieze. Horseshoe-shaped altars were discovered in Magnesia and in Priene. The altar in the Temple of Hera in Samos is the oldest. These altars were located in front of a temple, whereas the Altar of Zeus in Pergamon was an independent building dedicated to a god. It was also the highest of the three. The Altar of Zeus in Pergamon is an elegant structure where architectural, decorative and sculptural creations blend harmoniously.

The Upper Agora

The Upper Agora of the city was located on the terrace to the south of the Altar of Zeus. To conform to the topography of the land, it was built on an 'L'-shaped plan different from the customary rectangular or square-planned agoras. The ascending main street runs through the centre of the city and divides the area into two. At the southern and eastern edges, there are colonnades in the front and narrow shops in the back. Since the land where the southern colonnade was situated, sloped, a lower gallery resembling a basement was built on the side facing outward. The rooms of this lower gallery served as the depots of the shops at the upper level. In the western section of the agora, there is a small temple with its altar in the front. It was a prostyle temple of Doric and Ionic orders intermixed. The foundation of a structure resembling a temple was discovered nearby but it has not yet been identified.

Apart from the apsidal structure on the north-eastern corner, the Upper Agora was built in the Hellenistic era. The apsidal building was altered considerably in the Roman era. Although the function of such apsidal buildings is not known exactly, they were customarily found in the agoras in ancient cities. During certain hours of the day, court officials used to sit in these apses and help solve the problems of the people.

Approximately 100 metres to the south of the Upper Agora, a bath was built in conformity to the road ascending from below. Since all the sections except the tepidarium of the bath have collapsed completely, it is impossible to identify each section of this bath dated to the Roman era. The round tepidarium has an apsidal niche in the south. Preliminary borings at the site revealed the mosaic floor of another building which preceeded the bath.

29- Upper Agora.

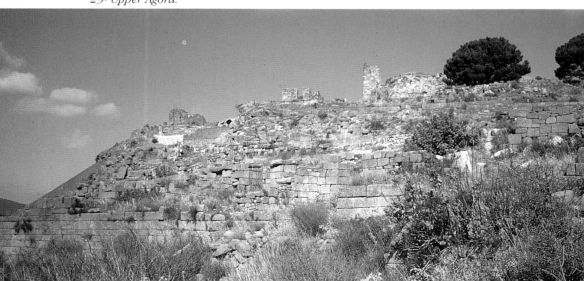

The Small Gymnasium
(the Bath, the Odeon, the Heroon)

A pproximately 150 metres below the bath by the main street with pavements, there is a complex of buildings, the excavation of which has been completed in recent years and a section of it has been restored. The complex consists of a bath, an odeon and a heroon. These three buildings under one roof were used as a gymnasium.

The bath was built between the main street and a narrow street running north from here. Just to the left of the entrance to the street, there is a square latrina. It is in a poor state of preservation. The sewer from the street passes under the latrina and joins the main sewer under the main street.

The frigidarium in the centre is the largest unit in the bath and resembles a courtyard. A few of its columns were re-erected later. The semicircular niche in the northern wall is the cold-water pool. The water storage area for the pool is located above the niche and it is in a good condition. The walls and the floor of the area were treated with water resistant plaster. The warmest room in the bath, the sudatorium, is located to the south of the frigidarium and it has a round plan. Below it is its stokehole, the entrance of which is on the main street. The two same sized structures in the west facing the street are the shops. In the east and adjoining the stokehole, there are three consecutive buildings which used to serve as the kitchens, provision depots, etc. of the heroon on the side. During restorations, the building by the street was roofed.

The frigidarium has two doors facing west. One of these doors gives access to the upper steps of the odeon. The seats of this rather small odeon are in an excellent state of preservation. Its orchestra is mesicircular, and the steps extending from the centre of the orchestra to the highest row of seats, divides the bow-shaped row of seats into two.

The marble hall adjacent to the odeon is the heroon of a Pergamene philanthropist named Diadoros Pasparos. It was also used as a cult room. The rectangular hall is directed south-east, and in the northern wall there is an apsidal niche with a triangular frontal. The cult statue of Diadoros Pasporos used to stand in the niche. Today, the head of the statue is in the Bergama Museum and a copy of it is in the hall. Since Diadoros Pasparos lived around 70 B.C., the odeon and the heroon have been dated. The walls and the floor of the heroon are covered with marble. Reliefs depicting cock-fights, as well as the star-decorated helmets, swords, armour and spears of the Dioscuri, were executed expertly on the panels hanging on the walls. Today, the copies of these panels can be seen on the walls. There used to be nine such panels on each one of the long side walls. Based on style, the reliefs are dated after the time of Diadoros Pasparos. It is known that, following the devastating earthquake in 17 A.D., Emperor Tiberium donated money to have the city reconstructed and he exempted Pergamon from taxes. It may be assumed

30- Main street.

31- Baths.

that during the reconstruction the damaged panels were replaced by new ones. During the restorations in recent years, a relief of Phallos, which symbolizes abundance and fertility, has been placed on the eastern facade. The heroon and the odeon were used up until the 4th century A.D..

32- Rooster Relief, from the decorations inside the Heroon

33- Heroon.

The Restaurant and the Shops

One or two-storeyed shops used to line both sides of the main street that started at the Eumenes II Gate at the southern foot of the acropolis and ascended toward the top of the hill. A few of the shops on the same side as the heroon have been excavated. The shop adjacent to the heroon has two sections. In the niche carved into rock in the northern wall of the rear section, there was a grill, and mixed in the soil in the niche, bones (such as those of chickens, partridges, pigs and others) were discovered. These finds indicate that there was an upretentious restaurant here. Adjoining this there is another unit consisting of two rooms which too must have been a restaurant. In later years, it was used for different purposes and damaged badly.

Large earthenware jars (pitnos) nestling in the holes carved into the soft rock under the floor, were found in the third shop by the street. These, and a counter extending outward on the wall facing the street, indicate that either wine or oil used to be sold in the third shop.

The Temple of Dionysus and the Hall with a Podium

A narrow staircase next to the eastern wall of the third shop, leads to the Temple of Dionysus situated on the upper terrace. In Pergamon, especially among the common people, worshipping Dionysus was quite popular. The worshippers used to gather here and organize ceremonies. Dionysus was known as the god of wine and nature, but the great power of Dionysus was not in nature itself, but in the relationship between nature and man. Knowing the secrets of nature, i.e. being deified, is an achievement yearned after by men, and Dionysus opens the door by wine and therefore by drunkenness. Members of the cult used to gather in the hall in the temple to get drunk and become ecstatic. The hall measures 24 by 10 metres, and a one metre high, 2.5 metre wide podium at the base of the walls, encircles the hall. The worshippers used to lie down on the podium, and eat the food and drink the wine set on the marble edge of the podium. Traces of the frescoes on the walls suggest that the walls of the hall were once decorated with frescoes of vines and grapes, since both were associated with Dionysus and wine. The altar in the middle and the niche in the northern wall were for Dionysus. Food and wine offered to the god used to be placed on the altar. Some of the wine was poured on the floor as a libation; the statue of Dionysus used to stand in the niche. There was a terrace with an earth floor in the front, and a fountain which was used for washing before each ceremony in the west, and service rooms in the east of the hall.

After the Temple of Dionysus, there is a narrow street sloping upward. On the east side of this street stand a partially restored large peristyle house and its bath. The house was constructed in the Hellenistic era, and later during the Roman era, it was enlarged and a bath was added on to it. As a result of the expansion, the road from the east wast left under the bath and its water depot.

The scanty remains seen by the main street indicate that here, there used to be shops with their houses in the back. Among these ruins there is a structure, the arch of which has been repaired. This is a fountain, and its water depot is carved into the rock behind it.

34- Stores.

35- Restaurant.

36- Dionysus cult area.

The Temple of Cybele (the Megalesion)

F ollowing the fountain, on the right side of the road there are
peristyle houses which are being excavated. These houses were
built in the Hellenistic era, and later in the 4th century A.D. they were
altered, and used either as workshops to produce bone objects, or
for other such similar purposes. In later years, different structures
were constructed over them, and therefore their original plan was
altered. About 100 metres down the road, also on the right side,
there is a large structure built like a peristyle house. Excavation of
the edifice was completed at the turn of the century. Since its mea-
surements exceed that of a regular house and its plan is different, it
must have been the temple of Cybele, the mother goddess. The
main temple of Cybele, the oldest goddess in Anatolia, is among the
Pessinus ruins in Sivrihisar near Ankara. The evolution of the mother
goddess during the Early Ages took place here. In Pessinus, people
worshipped a meteorite shaped like a Diopedes (goddess from the
sky) as the statue of Cybele for many years. This statue-like meteorite was sent to Rome by the Pergamene king Attalos I to help bring
victory at the end of the Carthaginian-Roman wars. With an impressive ceremony, Cybele was taken from her temple in Pessinus and

37- Agios Stratigos Fountain.

brought to Pergamon and placed in the Megalesion where the statue stayed for a year. Later it was taken to Rome. In the centre of the temple there is a large peristyle, and behind its eastern colonnade are the cult rooms.

38- Fountain with arches.

The Temenos of Demeter

A cross from the odeon on the terrace below the street, there is a complex of buildings. This is the temenos of Demeter and it is dated to before Philetairos' time. The structure was altered many times until the third century A.D. Although the actual site of the temple was not changed, the terrace was enlarged southward four times, in proportion to the expansion of Pergamon. The walls built in different styles demonstrate the extension of the terrace. According to the inscriptions, the temple and the temenos were dedicated to the memory of their mother Boa, by Philetairos and his brother Eumenes in the second half of the third century B.C., when extensive reconstruction were underway in Pergamon. On an arhcitectural fragment seen next to the temple, there is the inscription "Boa De-metri". During this same period, the columns of the prostyle temple of the Corinthian order were replaced by marble columns. The temple has five altars between its eastern facade and the propylon (the entrance), and the one in the front is the largest. The altar built in the Hellenistic era is decorated with palmette-shaped volutes in the corners, and it has been partially restored in recent years. Only the foundations of the other four altars are preserved. Colonnades are found on three sides of the temenos. The southern colonnade was built by Apollonis (241-197 B.C.), the wife of Attalos I. In order to enlarge the temenos, Apollonis had another wall built in front of the

39- Temenos of Demeter, general view.

40- Propylon, Temenos of Demeter.

Reconstruction of the Temenos of Demeter.

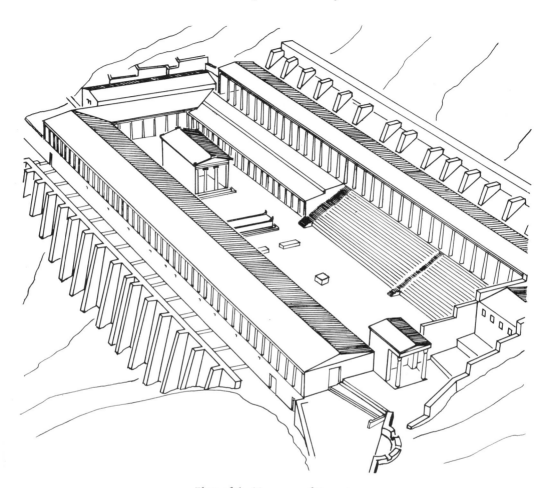

Plan of the Temenos of Demeter.

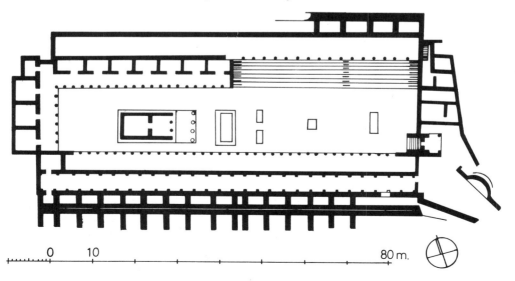

0   10   80 m.

41- Temenos of Demeter.

southern terrace wall and had the southern colonnade constructed on the old wall. This queen also built the propylon at the entrance to the temenos and its columns with palm leaf-decorated capitals. These columns were re-erected in recent years.

Rows of seats arranged like those in a stadium are seen along a section of the northern edge of the temenos, and these were used by the worshippers during ceremonies. At certain times during the year, festivals were organized at nights at the temenos for the god-

42- Propylon, Temenos of Demeter

43- Cornice with inscriptions.

44- The Great Altar, Temenos of Demeter.

45- *Temenos of Demeter.*

dess Demeter. The most famous festival was called Thesmophoria and it was attended only by the married ladies. Special prayers were held for Demeter and her daughter Persephone during the festival which took place in October. In a relief unearthed in the temenos, Demeter is depicted standing by the altar and holding a torch in her hands. The relief is on exhibit in the Bergama Museum. There is a round wishing-well in front of the entrance to the temenos. The women who came to wish for something or to attend the ceremonies, used to place their offerings such as pastries, chickens, pigs, etc, for Demeter and her daughter Persophone here. Most of the inscriptions seen in a row in front of the southern columns of the portico, were placed here by women as votives or thank-offerings. The fountain adjacent to the propylon, as in many other sacred precincts, was used for washing before a ceremony. The remains seen at the end of the road with a ramp to the north of the propylon, is assumed to be the remains of the prytaneion in Pergamon, but so far nothing to verify this has been unearthed.

The Temple of Hera and Its Temenos

The ruins seen spread over the wide area to the south of the Temenos of Demeter, belong to the Pergamene Gymnasium. The fifty metre high, narrow terrace at the north of the gymnasium was set aside for the goddess Hera. A side street from the Temenos of Demeter leads to the Temple of Hera. It is a prostyle temple in the Doric order, reached by a flight of wide steps. Narrow colonnades surround the structure, in the west of which there is a semicircular niche with steps for a statue. According to its dedicatory inscription, the temple was built by Attalos II (159-138 B.C.) and dedicated to Hera. Pieces belonging to a tall statue were discovered in the cella. It is assumed that the statue belonged either to Zeus, the husband of Hera, or to Attalos II. When viewed from below, the Temenos of Hera appeared in complete harmony with the gymnasium in front of it. This is why the temenos was constructed on this narrow terrace.

Before descending to the gymnasium from the Temenos of Hera, the foundation of a prostyle temple of a later date is seen in the west. According to a statue discovered in the course of excavations, the temple, dated to the early second century B.C., was dedicated to the god Asklepios.

46- Fountain, near the Propylon.

47- Gymnasium, general view.

The Gymnasium

The magnificent Gymnasium of Pergamon occupies a large area, and it was built on three separate terraces, one above the other. The uppermost terrace was reserved for older men, the middle one for young men and the lower one for children.

48- Gymnasium, general view.

49- Gymnasium, general view.

50- Auditorium of the Gymnasium.

The upper terrace was planned on a wider and more complex scale than the others. There is a courtyard in the centre surrounded by colonnades, and with baths in the east and west. In the middle of the western colonnade, there is a special area to bathe before and after the races. A fountain with an arch is situated by the western wall of the area and there are marble wash-basins along the southern and northern walls.

The first structure seen behind the northern colonnade is the auditorium. This semicircular building could seat 1,000 spectators and it resembles a small theatre. Its wooden podium has collapsed, but its five doors situated in the rear and on the side of the colonnade are well preserved. These doors were constructed just like those built in the stage buildings of the theatres. The door in the middle is wider and taller than the others. The vaulted structures on both sides of the auditorium were constructed to expand the seating area and to give the appearance of a theatre. The vault of the one in the east is in a good state of preservation. This structure was used as a cistern later. The traces of plaster seen on the walls belong to a later period. According to the inscriptions and the style of construction, the imperial hall of the gymnasium was the room with an apsidal niche at each end. It is located in the middle of the northern colonnade. The room with a niche in the northern wall, adjacent to the imperial hall, was the library. Both rooms were two-storeyed and made of coloured marble.

51- Wash-basins, lavatory of the gymnasium.

The bath located at the northern end of the gymnasium,is the largest and best preserved one in Pergamon. It is the whole width of the terrace of the gymnasium. Its eastern end rests against the city walls behind it,and its facade is in the direction of the eastern colonnade. There is an access to the bath from here, but the main entrance is at the eastern end of the northern colonnade. The columned courtyard-like room seen upon entering through the main entrance,is the frigidarium, from where two doorways lead into a hall with an apsidal northern wall, and to the long and narrow tepidarium (undressing area) which consists of two sections, and to the caldarium (hot area) next to the tepidarium. Just to the east of the structure there is a small city gate. A water distribution tank shaped like a bathtub and made of black marble, is seen on the road which enters the city through this gate. There are twelve holes in this tank which was used as a water-meter. Most probably, the largest hole was for the incoming water,and the others for the outgoing water. The water from the tank was distributed in measured amounts to the baths,and maybe also to the different sections of the gymnasium.

The bath located at the western end of the gymnasium is also in a good state of preservation. It is smaller than the other one. The narrow hallway at the southern side of the upper terrace of the gymnasium extends the whole length of the side (9,200 metres). It was used as an indoor running-track. A row of columns in the middle of

52- *Lavatory of the Gymnasium.*

53- Baths of the Gymnasium.

54- Frigidarium of the Baths.

55- Tepidarium of the Baths.

56- Hypocaust of the Caldarium, Baths.

the hall used to support the roof. On rainy days, races and training-sessions used to take place here. The windows in the southern wall were covered later.

The 150 metres long middle terrace of the gymnasium which was built in the reign of Eumenes II, is smaller than the upper terrace. Its features, characteristic of the time the gymnasium was built, are well preserved. At the eastern end of the running-track are the remains of a small temple and its altar. The prostyle temple was built in the Corinthian order and its altar is in front of the western entrance. Both are dated to the Hellenistic era. Names of the winners of races were carved on the walls of the temple. To the north of the middle terrace reserved for young men, there is a raised podium on which there is a colonnade. Small steps lead to the upper terrace from the colonnade, but the main set of stairs leading up to the upper terrace is at the eastern end. Two roads with steps (one at the eastern end and the other in the middle) lead to the lower terrace from the middle terrace. These roads were built during the Hellenistic period. When the city decreased in size, the city walls were built on these two terraces, and a round tower was constructed over the gate in the middle giving it a city-gate appearance. After descending the road with

57- Middle Gymnasium (section reserved for young men).

58- Gate with steps, between
the middle and lower gymnasium.

59- Middle Gymnasium.

steps, the remains of a 25 metres long nympheum (fountain) with a row of columns is seen on the right. The names of the winners used to be inscribed in the niches in the terrace walls. The running-track for children had a simple gate in the west and it has collapsed completely.

60- Water distribution tank, Gymnasium.

The Lower Agora

T he Lower Agora of Pergamon was smaller than its peers. The rectangular agora is flanked on all three sides by colonnades and small two-storeyed shops. The main street from the Eumenes II Gate follows the eastern and northern sides of the agora. Since the road is at a higher level, the second storeys of the shops in the northern colonnade face the road. The first storeys of the shops had to face outward, because the land sloped at the end of the southern colonnade where the terrace ended.

In the centre of the agora, there is a cistern which was supplied by water from the large cistern in Consul Attalos' house in the north via earthenware pipes. In the course of excavations, a group of inscriptions pertaining to the rules and regulations in the city was discovered in the agora. These, and the andesite shots unearthed in the arsenals are exhibited here.

There is a nympheum (fountain) with columns to the north-east of the agora. It has been repaired and brought here, because the area it was situated in will be flooded during the repairing of a dam on the eastern side of the acropolis. The fountain known as the Agios Stratigos Fountain has a pool and columns of the Doric order. It was built in the Hellenistic era and repaired in the Byzantine period.

61- Agios Stratigos Fountain (moved from the dam site).

62- Pools, Red courtyard (temple for the Egyptian gods).

63- Red Courtyard (facade of the temple for the Egyptian gods).

The House of Consul Attalos

On the terrace to the north of the agora, there is a peristyle house. It was built in the Hellenistic era and altered in the Roman period. The columns surrounding the peristyle are two-tiered. The lower columns are of the Doric order and the upper ones of the Ionic order. The main unit of the house is the large hall at the western side of the peristyle. The hall was used by men during meetings and feasts. The bust of Attalos, which is now in Berlin, used to stand on the herm-shaped base in this room. The inscription on the base states 'Consul Attalos invites his friends to enjoy life with him'. A section of the house has been roofed to protect it.

The Red Courtyard
(the Temple for the Egyptian Gods)

The city walls lost their importance after Pax Romana, and the city of Pergamon expanded down toward the plain at the foot of the acropolis. Among the monumental structures built during this time, the Stadium, the New Theatre, the Amphitheatre and the Temple dedicated to the Egyptian gods (the Red Courtyard) are the most important. So far, only the Red Courtyard has been excavated. Since it was constructed of red bricks, it is popularly known in Bergama as the Red Courtyard.

64- Red Courtyard (temple for the Egyptian gods, view from the south.)   *65- Caryatid.*

66- *Caryatid.*

A section of the temenos is under the city of Bergama today. The temenos measured 100 by 200 metres, and the main temple was 60 metres long and 26 metres wide. Although its upper section has collapsed, the walls standing today measure 19 metres in height. The domed structures on each side of the eastern end of the temple, are a few of the rare domed structures which were built in the Roman era and have survived up to the present day; the one in the north serves as a mosque and the other one as the storage room of the museum. There are colonnades on three sides of the main structure. Instead of columns, two back-to-back caryatids were used. Large sections of a few of these are in the vicinity of the temple. One of these was a male figure and the other a female, and they resembled in style, the statues of the Egyptian gods. The caryatids were not made of a single block of marble, but the arms and the bust of each one were built separately and then fitted into place on the trunk. Since these figures were built like the Egyptian statues, and there were water canals and pools in front of the side colonnades, it is assumed that the temple was built for the Egyptian gods. It must have been dedicated to the gods Isis and Serapis.

The gate at the entrance of the temple is 14 metres high and 7 metres wide. Behind the threshold made from a single piece of marble, there is a marble 'couch'. A shallow pool and a well are located in the

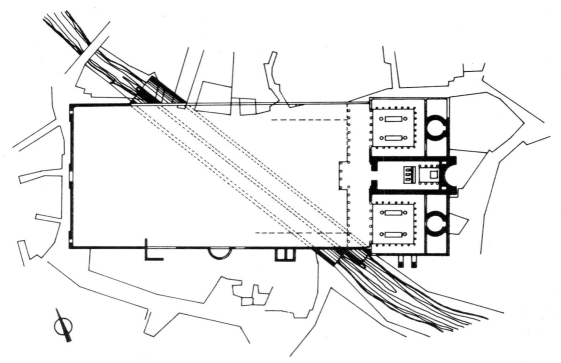

Plan of the Temple of the Egyptian Gods.

centre of the structure. A large statue of either a god or a goddess used to stand on the base seen on the podium in front of the apsidal wall at the eastern end. According to the size of the temple and the statue base, the statue must have been 10 metres high. The priests used to enter the statue through the passage under the podium and preach through the mouth of the statue. There are two-storeyed galleries supported by marble columns on all four sides of the structure inside. There was a window above each of the five niches in the side walls, and the temple received adequate light through these windows. However, since there were no windows in the rear section, it was always darker there. There was a narrow staircase on each side of the apsidal wall. One of these led up to the inner gallery and the other to the roof. The extant fragments do not give enough clues to show us out how the structure was roofed.

The Red Courtyard was built in the years of Emperor Hadrian, and it was completely covered by marble in the Early Ages. Since the Selinus river ran under the area where the temple was situated, two vaulted tunnels, each measuring 9 metres in diameter, had to be built under the temenos. These tunnels are in a good state of preservation. The Roman bridges on both sides of the tunnel are still used today. During the Byzantine period, a church dedicated to St. John was built in the main edifice. Today, only one or two metre high walls remain from the church.

The Amphitheatre

The hill between the acropolis and the asklepeion was densely populated during the Roman period. There is a Roman theatre on the side of the hill overlooking the plain below, an amphitheatre on the northern side where a small stream runs, and a stadium on the extension of the hill toward the acropolis. These have not yet been excavated. The large wide arches and a section of their supporting walls are still in good shape. The diameter of the theatre, built over a stream, is 60 metres. When needed, the empty area in the middle used to be filled with water, and therefore the plays requiring water scenes were performed more realistically.

67- Amphitheatre (not excavated).

68- Amphitheatre (not excavated).

69- Roman Theatre (not excavated).

The Asklepeion

A road to the left of the entrance to the city of Bergame leads to the asklepeion, which is similar to those in Epidaurus and Kos. According to Pausanias, the earliest Temple of Asklepios in Pergamon was built in the 4th century B.C. Most of the remains seen today date back to the reign of Emperor Hadrian. Its sacred road started at the Roman theatre, which used to stand at today's Viran Kapı (the Ruined Gate), traversed the Roman city and reached the asklepeion. This sacred road, called Via Tecta, was 820 metres long and 18.14 metres wide. It was excavated by Erich Boehringer in 1967. The last 40 metres of the road was altered in the reign of Emperor Hadrian and turned into a street lined with columns. The pavements were covered with big blocks of andesite. As indicated by the pavements, a canal stretches through the middle of the road. On the southern side of the street there is a round mausoleum, the top section of which has collapsed. It was built in the reign of Emperor Augustus. Its tomb is square and its door faces south. A fountain built in later years, a few structures still being excavated and a road, are seen across from the mausoleum. Valuable statues dating to the Hellenistic period were discovered in different sections of the road during excavations. Via Tecta stretches as far as the propylon of the asklepeion. The propylon was built by Claudius Charax (131-161 A.D.) in the reign of Antonius Pius and presented to the city. Sources indicate that Claudius Charax was an historian and a consul. On the street

70- Asklepeion, Sacred Road (Via Tecta).

71- Altar in the Propylon, Asklepeion.

72- Northern gallery, Asklepeion.

side, the propylon has a courtyard, three sides of which are occupied by colonnades of the Corinthian order. On the side facing the asklepeion, the propylon has a pediment supported by four columns and a flight of stairs at the entrance. Today, the pediment is located on the west side of the courtyard, and the two side acroteria of the pediment which demonstrate excellent workmanship, are in the Bergame Museum. One of these depicts a "Nike" which is the symbol of the museum.

In the wide area seen after the propylon, many different structures were built between the 4th century B.C. and the second century A.D. Excavations revealed eighteen different construction phases in this time period. Colonnades occupy three sides of the area, and the east side was set aside for buildings. Just to the left of the propylon there is a cult niche, and next to it a large imperial hall. The hall was also used as a library. The tall statue of Hadrian, today exhibited in the Bergama Museum, used to stand in the niche in the eastern wall of the library. Since the emperor was deified, be was depicted naked. According to the inscription on the base of the statue, someone named Melitine had the statue made and dedicated it to Emperor Hadrian. On the walls of the hall which were covered with coloured marble in the reign of Emperor Hadrian, the traces of the brackets on which the bookshelves were mounted are still visible today. As in all the libraries of the Early Ages, the hall had double-layered walls to protect the books against humidity.

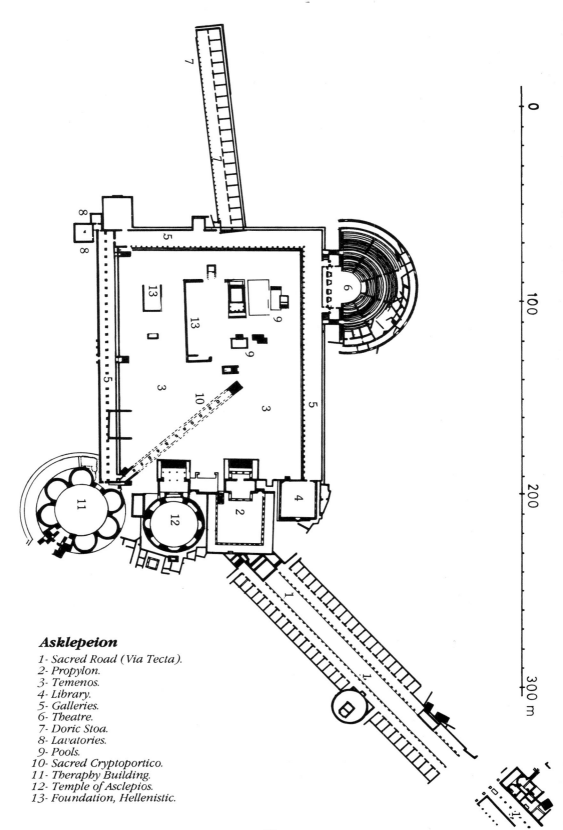

Asklepeion

1- Sacred Road (Via Tecta).
2- Propylon.
3- Temenos.
4- Library.
5- Galleries.
6- Theatre.
7- Doric Stoa.
8- Lavatories.
9- Pools.
10- Sacred Cryptoportico.
11- Theraphy Building.
12- Temple of Asclepios.
13- Foundation, Hellenistic.

73- *Columns of the northern gallery, Asklepeion.*

74- *Asklepeion, general view.*

The northern colonnade of the courtyard has been repaired in recent years and it is in a good state of preservation. The tall slender columns have capitals of the Ionic order. About ten of the columns on the library side had collapsed during the devastating carthquake in Western Anatolia in 175 A.D. and were replaced by columns of the Corinthian order. These new columns were shorter than the others so their bases were raised. According to the custom in Pergamon and in many other cities, the floor of the colonnade was made of earth. The wall in the back was covered with decorative marble to create an unusual appearance. The small theatre where concerts and plays were staged is at the other end of the colonnade. Concerts and plays were part of the treatment administered in the asklepeion. The theatre could seat 3,500 spectators. there was a low vault supported by small Ionic columns behind the highest row of seats, the theatre also had a marble box reserved for dignitaries. The stage building is three-storeyed. Therefore, the theatre was typical of theatres built in the Roman age.

Just like the northern colonnade, the western colonnade of the courtyard was also built in the Ionic order. A stoa extending towards the hills in the back was discovered in the course of excavations in

75- *Theatre, Asklepeion.*

1967, and a section of it has been restored. It is assumed that the stoa, which is in the Doric order, was built to connect some of the buildings to the west of the asklepeion. Only andesite was used in the construction of the stoa. On the corner where the western colonnade and the southern colonnade meet, there are two lavatories and an impressive hall. The smaller lavatory was for ladies and the larger one for men. The one reserved for ladies was plain and served seventeen, whereas the one for men was ornamented with decorative marble and served forty. The hall next to the lavatories was used during meetings and conferences. The four Corinthian columns in the middle of the hall were built to carry the heavy roof. According to a theory, the hall which is completely plated with marble, was built without a roof to receive light, and fresh air.

The southern colonnade of the asklepeion is two-storeyed. The first storey stands on a rock and has a low ceiling. The thick andesite columns supported the upper gallery. Nothing remains from the upper gallery which was built in the Ionic order.

The treatment given in the asklepeion was based on natural sources. Many inscriptions unearthed during the excavations describe the methods of treatment. Aelius Aristides, the orator, stayed

76- Theatre, Asklepeion.

77- Doric Stoa, Asklepeion.

here for thirteen years around the middle of the second century and received treatment. These years which coincide with the reign of Emperor Hadrian, constitute the golden age of the asklepeion. The most famous physicians of the Early Ages, such as Satyros and Calinos,lived during this period. Besides faith-healing, self-suggestion, psychology, sports, mud baths, and baths in the waters from the sacred springs were the main methods of treatment. The three pools seen in front of the theatre were used for water baths. The pools made of marble had steps to facilitate getting in and out. Water from the sacred spring still runs today. Analysis of the water has shown that it has enough radioactivity to be effective in treatments. The belief that death (Hades) could not enter the asklepeion,made the patients feel better psychologically as soon as they stepped into the sacred area. The sick usually walked barefooted on the sacred road to reach the sacred area. The belief that each step taken carried them further away from death,must have been the beginning of the treatment. After they bathed in the pools, the patients walked through the cryptoportico just beyond the sacred spring, to reach the treatment buildings. The 80 metres long cryptoportico was built below ground level, and inside it was very quiet and dim. Water from the sacred spring ran down the steps creating small falls, and the sound of it enhanced the mystic atmosphere. The round structure (26.5

78- *Cryptoportico, Asklepeion.*

79- **Therapy Building.**

metres in diameter) at the end of the gallery was the treatment building, and it had two storeys. The upper storey has collapsed completely. In the niches found in the first storey, there were beds where the patients slept. The patients used to pray until they fell asleep; their dreams were interpreted by the experienced physicians in the asklepeion. One of the doors of the structure opened onto a wide terrace where the patients sunbathed.

The main building of the asklepeion is the temple dedicated to the god of healing, Asklepios. The round temple (23.85 metres in diameter) situated between the treatment building and the propylon, was built before the treatment building by Consul L. Cuspius Pactumeus Rufinos in 150 A.D. and presented to the city of Pergamon. Its

80- Therapy Building.

entrance has steps and columns. It resembled the Pantheon in Rome which had been built twenty years before. The columns seen on the sides of the cornered and curved niches inside, support the dome. Statues of the gods and goddesses associated with healing occupied the niches. In the big niche opposite the entrance was the statue of Asklepios.

The foundations seen in the area in front of the theatre, are dated to the Hellenistic era. These are the remains of pools, temples and sleeping areas. The temples were dedicated to Asklepios Soter, Apollon Kalliteknos and goddess Hygieia. The remains seen in front of the southern colonnade belong to the pool where Aristides, the orator, used to bathe, around 150 A.D.

81- Tumulus in the plain.

82- Tiled minaret, Seljuk.

The treasures unearthed in the course of archaeological excavations in the city, and those brought in from the other ancient cities in the region, are displayed in the Bergama Museum which was founded in 1936. Until then, most of the finds were taken to Berlin, and a few were taken to the Archaeological Museum in Istanbul.

In the garden by the entrance to the museum grounds at Bergama, marble grave steles (dated to the first century B.C. and the second century A.D.) unearthed in the region, particularly in the East Lydian cities, and friezes, column capitals, and various other architectural fragments brought in from the acropolis are displayed. Some of the sarcophagi and the ostotechs seen in the garden were discovered in the necropolis at the foot of the acropolis.

The marble sarcophagus seen in front of the gate upon entrance into the inner courtyard, is dated to the period when the Çömlekçiler (pottery makers) district located by the Cetius river was a necropolis (first century A.D.). Inside, there is another sarcophagus made of lead, and it contains the burnt skeleton. It is one of those rare sarcophagi which was discovered unopened. It belonged to a boy approximately eleven to twelve years old. A toy bird on wheels, a miniature baked clay hearth, Myrina figurines, and a coin belonging to the second half of the first century A.D. were discovered in the sarcophagus. Under the eaves in the middle garden, the inscriptions, reliefs, friezes, and the statues discovered in the Temenos of Athena, the Temenos of Demeter and the Gymnasium are displayed. Of the two acroteria in the centre, the one on the right depicts a flying "Nike" and it comes from the pediment of the propylon of the asklepeion. The cauldron seen in front of this was used for cremation and it was discovered in the Diadoros Pasparos Heroon on the acropolis. Parts of the cauldron are made of a different kind of marble. These are the traces of repairs which took place in ancient times. The marble statues exhibited under the eaves on the museum side, are the immortal treasures of the school of Pergamene sculpture. The torso of Hermes, seen on the right, displays excellent craftsmanship. In the south, there is a model of the Zeus Altar and next to it, there is a marble panel on which a sacrificial bull being led to the altar is depicted.

83- Nike, Acroteria, Propylon of the Asklepeion.   *84- Frieze, 2nd century B.C.*

85- Early Roman stele.

86- Frieze with garlands, 1st century B.C.

87- Grave stele, 1st century A.D.

88- Ostotech, 1st century A.D.

89- Frieze with masks, 1st century B.C.

The statue made of soft marble, seen at the entrance to the covered section of the museum, belongs to the 6th century B.C. and was discovered in Pitane (today's Çandarlı). In the course of excavations in Çandarlı, besides this statue, important funerary gifts which shed light on the archaeology of the region were discovered. In the 6th century B.C. when Pergamon had not yet developed, Pitane was an important city by the sea.

The mosaic seen in the middle of the first hall on the right, is called the "Mosaic with a Medusa". In the centre of the mosaic there is a Medusa head, and at the perimeter there are colourful geometric ornamentations. The mosaic is dated to the third century A.D.

In the showcase by the right wall, Roman figurines discovered in Pergamon are displayed. The one hanging from the ceiling of the showcase is a puppet and many of these were unearthed in Pergamon. There is a group statue of two next to the above showcase. The statue depicting a young slim man is of Dionysus, and the other is of the satyr Silenos. The upper parts of the statues are broken. As we can recognize from the other statues of the group found in other museums, and from the baked clay objects with reliefs discovered in Pergamon, a drunken Dionysus is walking with his arm on Silenos' shoulder. The bust depicting a man's head with his hair covered, belongs to Emperor Caracalla. When Caracalla came to the asklepeion in Pergamon for treatment, he had his statue erected.

The marble panels seen by the mosaic, are the wall panels of the Diadoros Pasparos Heroon. Weapons, a cock-fight and a Dioscuri helmet are depicted on three different panels. Since the Dioscuri became the stars of the constellation Gemini after they died, a star is depicted on the helmet.

90- Grave stele, 2nd century A.D.

91- Cybele, statue and altar, 2nd century B.C.

92- Phaloss.

93- *Middle courtyard, Bergama Museum.*

    Among the statues by the wall, the one in the middle belongs to Emperor Hadrian. He is depicted naked and standing. The statue was discovered in front of the niche in the library during the excavations in the asklepeion. The statue of the emperor had been erected in the asklepeion in gratitude for his help. The statue seen towards the left, depicts Tyche carrying the fertility horn (cornucopia) and it belongs to the first century A.D. The busts that come after the statue of Tyche belong to famous philosophers and other personalities who helped the city of Pergamon, and they were made in different periods.

94- *Marble cauldron, 1st century B.C.*

95- *Column capital, Byzantine.*

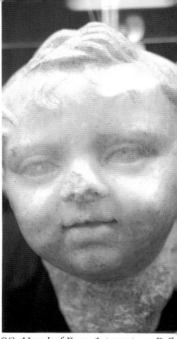

96- Acroteria, Propylon.

97- Nike, acroteria of the Propylon.

98- Head of Eros, 1st century B.C.

99- Hellenistic statues, Middle courtyard.

100- Curos, 6th century B.C.

101- Emperor Hadrian, 2nd century A.D.

At the beginning of the hallway that leads to the second hall, there is a showcase in which oil-lamps, and negative moulds used in making oil-lamps and appliquéd ceramics, are displayed. Positive prints used to be made from negative moulds and were then appliquéd on to the bowls. These were mostly Dionysiac and erotic in design. In Hellenistic times, this type of appliquéd ceramic was either used or produced mostly in Pergamon. Many such bowls were discovered in the potteries located in the vicinity of Celius (Kestel) river. In the other showcase, the coins unearthed in Pergamon are displayed in chronological order. Coins belonging to the Pergamene Kingdom are the most valuable.

Various containers discovered during the excavations in Kestel are displayed in the showcase by the wall on the left. The potteries in Kestel were used from the third century B.C. until the 5th century A.D., and most of the pots produced here were exported. In the first small showcase by the wall on the right, marble statuettes of Cybele are exhibited. One of these statuettes dating to the Kingdom of Pergamon was discovered on the acropolis, and the other one was found by the Kestel river. Cybele was always worshipped in Pergamon. The baked clay statuettes seen in the other showcase in the same row, were made in Myrina. These baked clay statuettes were discovered in Pergamon. During the Hellenistic and early Roman eras, Myrina was an important centre of baked clay statuette production. Most of the statuettes produced here were used as funerary gifts in Pergamon. In another showcase by the southern wall, painted figurines are displayed. In one of the showcases on the left side of the hall, baked clay objects belonging to the Byzantine era, and in the other showcase, the earliest Yortan containers (the black ones)

102- Hermes, 1st century B.C.

103- Statue of a woman, 1st century B.C.

104- Relief from the Heroon

105- Glass containers, 2nd century A.D.

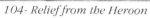

106- Stele with Helios, 2nd century A.D.

107- Tyche statue, 1st century A.D.

108- Ceramic containers, Hellenistic.

109- Baked-clay statuette, 1st century B.C.

110- Gold Ear (votive offering), Hellenistic.

owned by the Bergama Museum, are exhibited. The large showcase in the middle contains cups such as craters, scyphi, and cantari, which were all made in Pergamon, most of them during the Hellenistic era. The big crater in the middle is decorated in the "Western Slope" style. Since this type of cup was first discovered on the western slopes of the acropolis in Athens, they were given this name. Yet, according to some theories, the Western Slope ceramic-ware was produced in Pergamon first. In another showcase by the southern wall, ceramic-ware produced in the city of Grineion is displayed. These cups decorated with geometric designs, were discovered in the course of excavations initiated by the Bergama Museum. They are dated to the 6th century B.C.

111- Baked-clay child figurine, 1st century B.C.

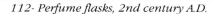

112- Perfume flasks, 2nd century A.D.

113- Aphrodite, 1st century B.C.

There is also an Ethnographical Hall in the Bergama Museum, and the entrance to the hall is from the middle courtyard. Here, regional costumes, weaves such as rugs, kilims, bags and other handiwork are displayed.

Glossary

Acroterium: The figures or ornaments crowning the apex or the lower angles of a pediment.

Agora: Market-place.

Architrave: A lintel supported by columns.

Caryatid: Figure of a maiden replacing a column.

Cella: The main chamber of a Greek temple containing the cult statue.

Crepidoma: The stepped platform of a Greek temple.

Odeon: A roofed building in which rehearsals and musical contests were held.

Palaestra: A training school for all kinds of physical exercises.

Pediment: The triangular termination of a pitched roof.

Peripteros: A temple surrounded by a row of columns.

Peristyle: A courtyard surrounded by colonnades.

Prostylos: A temple preceeded by a porch with columns in front.

Stoa: A long covered hall with columns in front.

Propylon: The entrance gate building of a precinct or a sacred enclosure.

Temenos: A sacred precinct with one or more temples.

Bibliography

Akurgal E., Ancient Civilization and Ruins of Turkey. Istanbul 1984
Akurgal E., Eski İzmir. Ankara 1983
Bayatlı O., Bergama Tarihi 1-3. Istanbul 1949/51
Bean G.E., Aegean Turkey. London 1966
Bosch M.E., Bergama Krallık Hanedanının Şeceresi. Istanbul
Bosch M.E., Hellenizm Tarihinin Ana Hatları. Istanbul
Davesne A., Remarques Sur la Grande Frise de L'autel de
    Pergame. Revues des Etudes Anciennes 1977
Deubner O., Das Asklepieion von Pergamon. Berlin 1938
Erhat A., Mitoloji Sözlüğü. Istanbul 1972
Eriş E., Bergama Uygarlık Tarihi. İzmir 1979
Felten F., Römische Architektur in Pergamon. Berlin 1938
Gökovalı Ş., Pergam. İzmir
Hansen E., The Attalids of Pergamon. London 1972
Kasper S., Zum Großen Altar der Demeter-Terrasse.
    Pergamenische Forschüngen. Berlin 1971
Mansel A.M., Ege ve Yunan Tarihi. Ankara 1966
Radt W., Bergama. Istanbul 1984
Radt W., Pergamon Vorbericht Über die Kampagne 1980. AA 1981
Radt W.-Rombock U., Vorbericht Über die Kampagne 1975. AA 1976
Ziegenaus O.-Luca G.d., Das Asklepieion. Berlin 1968-1975

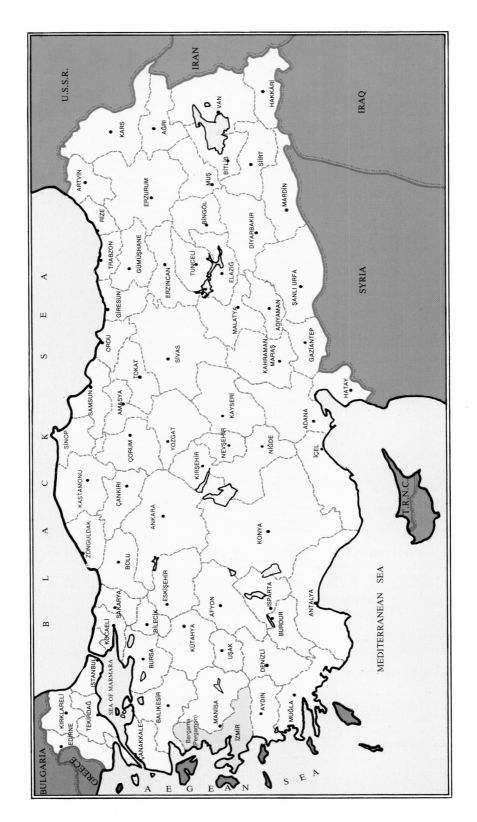

Map of Turkey.

U.S.S.R.

IRAN

IRAQ

SYRIA

BULGARIA

GREECE

B L A C K   S E A

A E G E A N   S E A

SEA OF MARMARA

MEDITERRANEAN SEA

T.R.N.C.

VAN

HAKKÂRİ

KARS

AĞRI

ARTVİN

ERZURUM

SİİRT

BİTLİS

MUŞ

BİNGÖL

DİYARBAKIR

MARDİN

RİZE

TRABZON

GÜMÜŞHANE

TUNCELİ

ELAZİĞ

ŞANLI URFA

ERZİNCAN

GİRESUN

ORDU

MALATYA

ADIYAMAN

GAZİANTEP

SİVAS

KAHRAMAN MARAŞ

TOKAT

AMASYA

HATAY

SAMSUN

SİNOP

KAYSERİ

ADANA

YOZGAT

NEVŞEHİR

NİĞDE

İÇEL

ÇORUM

KASTAMONU

KIRŞEHİR

ÇANKIRI

ANKARA

KONYA

ZONGULDAK

BOLU

ESKİŞEHİR

ISPARTA

SAKARYA

BİLECİK

AFYON

BURDUR

ANTALYA

KOCAELİ

KÜTAHYA

İSTANBUL

BURSA

UŞAK

DENİZLİ

KIRKLARELİ

TEKİRDAĞ

BALIKESİR

MANİSA

AYDIN

MUĞLA

EDİRNE

ÇANAKKALE

Bergama (Pergamon)

İZMİR

109

PUBLICATION LIST

TURKEY (BN) *(In English, French, German, Italian, Spanish, Dutch)*
ANCIENT CIVILIZATIONS AND RUINS OF TURKEY *(In English)*
ISTANBUL (B) *(In English, French, German, Italian, Spanish, Japanese)*
ISTANBUL (ORT) *(In English, French, German, Italian, Spanish)*
ISTANBUL (BN) *(In English, French, German, Italian, Spanish, Japanese)*
MAJESTIC ISTANBUL *(In English, German)*
TURKISH CARPETS *(In English, French, German, Italian, Spanish, Japanese)*
TURKISH CARPETS *(In English, German)*
THE TOPKAPI PALACE *(In English, French, German, Italian, Italian, Spanish, Japanese, Turkish)*
HAGIA SOPHIA *(In English, French, German, Italian, Spanish)*
THE KARİYE MUSEUM *(In English, French, German, Italian, Spanish)*
ANKARA *(In English, French, German, Italian, Spanish, Turkish)*
Unique CAPPADOCIA *(In English, French, German, Italian, Spanish, Japanese, Turkish)*
CAPPADOCIA (BN) *(In English, French, German, Italian, Spanish, Dutch, Turkish)*
EPHESUS *(In English, French, German, Italian, Spanish, Japanese)*
EPHESUS (BN) *(In English, French, German, Italian, Spanish, Dutch)*
APHRODISIAS *(In English, French, German, Italian, Spanish, Turkish)*
THE TURQUOISE COAST OF TURKEY *(In English)*
PAMUKKALE (HIERAPOLIS) *(In English, French, German, Italian, Spanish, Dutch, Japanese, Turkish)*
PAMUKKALE (BN) *(In English, French, German, Italian, Spanish)*
PERGAMON *(In English, French, German, Italian, Spanish, Japanese)*
LYCIA (AT) *(In English, French, German)*
KARIA (AT) *(In English, French, German)*
ANTALYA (BN) *(In English, French, German, Italian, Dutch, Turkish)*
PERGE *(In English, French, German)*
ASPENDOS *(In English, French, German)*
ALANYA *(In English, French, German, Turkish)*
The Capital of Urartu: VAN *(In English, French, German)*
TRABZON *(In English, French, German, Turkish)*
TURKISH COOKERY *(In English, French, German, Italian, Spanish, Dutch, Japanese, Turkish)*
NASREDDİN HODJA *(In English, French, German, Italian, Spanish, Japanese)*
TÜRKÇE-JAPONCA KONUŞMA KILAVUZU *(Japanese-Turkish)*
ANADOLU UYGARLIKLARI *(Turkish)*

MAPS

TURKEY (NET), TURKEY (ESR), TURKEY (WEST)
TURKEY (SOUTH WEST), ISTANBUL, MARMARİS,
ANTALYA-ALANYA, ANKARA, İZMİR, CAPPADOCIA

NET® BOOKSTORES

ISTANBUL
Galleria Ataköy, Sahil Yolu, 34710 Ataköy - Tel: (9-1) 559 09 50
Ramada Hotel, Ordu Caddesi, 226, 34470 Laleli - Tel: (9-1) 513 64 31
İZMİR
Cumhuriyet Bulvarı, 142/B, 35210 Alsancak - Tel: (9-51) 21 26 32